Published by Pebble, an imprint of Capstone
1710 Roe Crest Drive, North Mankato, Minnesota 56003
www.capstonepub.com

Copyright © 2026 by by Capstone. All rights reserved. No part of this publication may be reproduced in whole or in part, or stored in a retrieval system, or transmitted in any form or by any means, electronic, mechanical, photocopying, recording, or otherwise, without written permission of the publisher.

Library of Congress Cataloging-in-Publication Data is available on the Library of Congress website.
ISBN: 9798875224621 (hardcover)
ISBN: 9798875224492 (paperback)
ISBN: 9798875224584 (ebook PDF)

Summary: An introduction to black widow spiders, including their habitat, hunting habits, life cycle, and more.

Editorial Credits
Editor: Ashley Kuehl; Designer: Bobbie Nuytten; Media Researcher: Svetlana Zhurkin; Production Specialist: Whitney Schaefer

Image Credits
Capstone: Kay Fraser (spiderweb), cover and throughout; Getty Images: EdwardSnow, 16, MediaProduction, 19, stphillips, 6, 10, 18; Newscom: ZUMA Press/Kike Calvo, 11; Shutterstock: All Write studio (spiderweb), 4, 8, 14, 18, Chase D'animulls (spider), cover, back cover, 1, Jay Ondreicka, 4, 15, lighTTrace Studio, 5, Malpolon, 9, phonecat, 7, Sari Oneal, 13, Sviktoria, 20, Wirestock Creators, 14, 17

Any additional websites and resources referenced in this book are not maintained, authorized, or sponsored by Capstone. All product and company names are trademarks™ or registered® trademarks of their respective holders.

Printed and bound in China. 6274

TABLE OF CONTENTS

All About Black Widows 4

The Cycle of Life 8

A Sticky Web 14

Don't Touch! 18

    Draw a Spider 20

    Spider Jokes 21

    Glossary 22

    Read More 23

    Internet Sites 23

    Index 24

    About the Author 24

Words in **bold** are in the glossary.

ALL ABOUT BLACK WIDOWS

See that spider? She has a red or orange spot on her belly. The spot looks like an **hourglass**. This spider is a black **widow**.

A black widow has eight legs. It has a two-part body. Females are shiny black. Males are brown or gray.

Females are about 1.5 inches (3.8 centimeters) long. Males are much smaller. They may have red and white stripes on their sides.

Widow spiders live all over the world. They nest in dark places near the ground. A log or a hole makes a good home. Or you may find them in a shed or a house. Each spider lives alone.

THE CYCLE OF LIFE

In summer, a female black widow finds a mate. But look out! If she is hungry, she may eat him. This is how the black widow got its name.

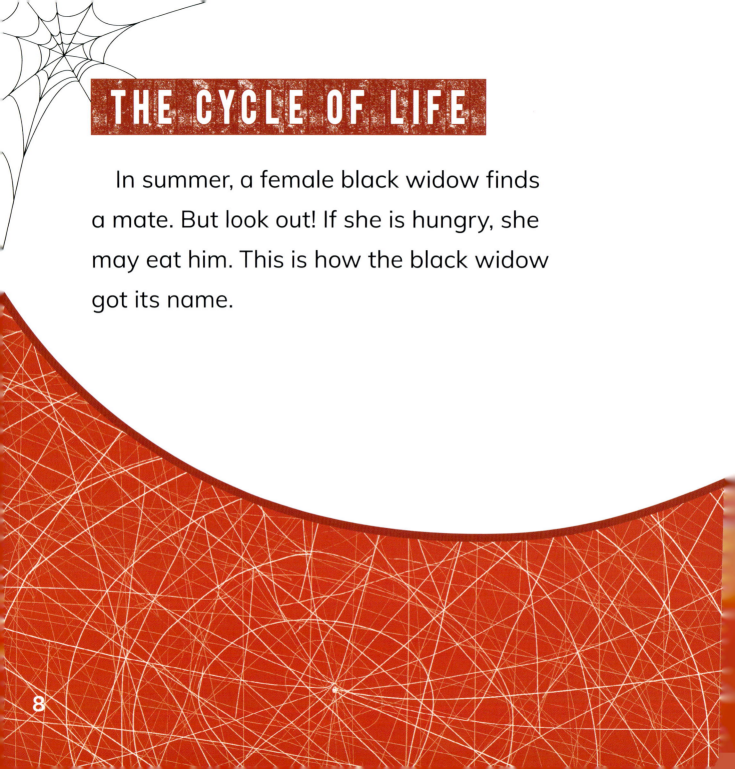

The female lays more than 200 eggs. They are in a white egg sac. It sticks to her web. She keeps her eggs safe. In a few weeks, the eggs will **hatch**.

Some of the young spiders eat one another. **Predators** kill some too. Birds and insects eat black widows.

Each baby spider spins a strand of **silk**. It acts like a balloon. The wind carries it away. The spider will find a new home when it lands.

A STICKY WEB

Black widows eat bugs. They eat other spiders too. They use their webs to catch food.

A black widow's web looks messy. The silk is very sticky. But the spider does not get stuck. Oil coats its legs. It waits for its **prey**.

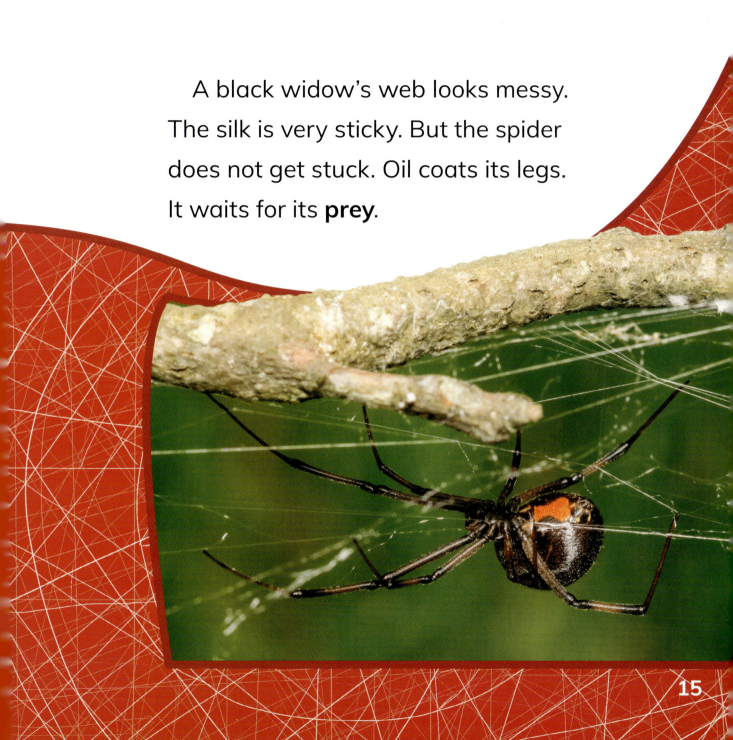

Zing! The spider feels its web move. It rushes over. Dinner is here! It sinks in its **fangs**. **Venom** flows into the bug's body. It cannot move.

The spider wraps the bug in silk. The silk is as strong as steel! The bug's body breaks down. The spider sips up the juice. Now it will rest and wait for its next meal.

DON'T TOUCH!

If you see a black widow, stay away! The spider may hide or play dead. But it can bite if it feels trapped. Females will bite to protect their eggs.

If a black widow bites you, call a doctor. They can give you **antivenom**. It will fight the poison.

DRAW A SPIDER

Draw a black widow spider. Color the hourglass red. Label the parts of its body. Here is a list you can use:

- head
- fangs
- hourglass marking
- legs

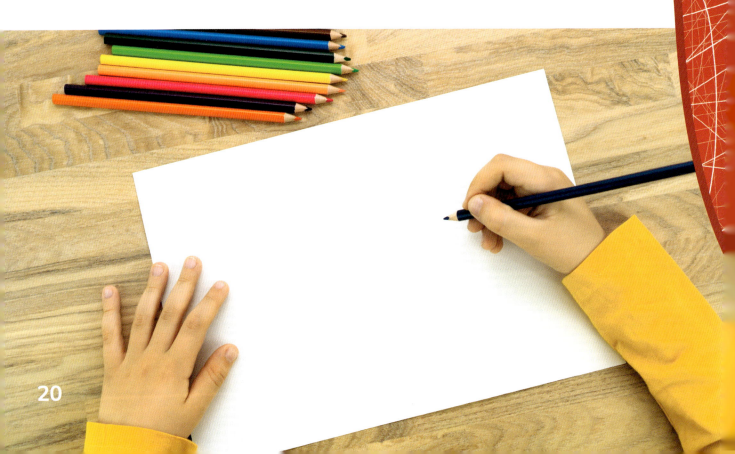

SPIDER JOKES

Why are spiders great at playing baseball?

They catch all the flies.

What do you get if you cross a spider and an ear of corn?

Cobwebs!

What do you call an undercover bug?

a spy-der

Why did the spider buy a computer?

So he could check his website!

GLOSSARY

antivenom (AN-ti-VEN-uhm)—a medicine that fights venom

fang (FANG)—the biting part of a spider's mouth

hatch (HACH)—to break out of an egg

hourglass (OUR-glas)—a tool for measuring time

predator (PRED-uh-tur)—an animal that hunts other animals for food

prey (PRAY)—an animal hunted by another animal for food

silk (SILK)—long, thin threads made by a spider

venom (VEN-uhm)—a poisonous liquid produced by some animals

widow (WID-oh)—a woman whose spouse or partner has died

READ MORE

Anthony, William. *Black Widow Spider*. New York: Enslow Publishing, 2022.

Culliford, Amy. *Black Widow Spider*. New York: Crabtree Publishing, 2022.

Murray, Julie. *Black Widow Spiders*. Minneapolis: Abdo Publishing, 2020.

INTERNET SITES

A–Z Animals: 10 Incredible Black Widows Spider Facts
a-z-animals.com/blog/10-incredible-black-widow-spider-facts/

Nemours KidsHealth: Hey, a Black Widow Spider Bit Me!
kidshealth.org/en/kids/black-widow.html

National Geographic Kids: Black Widow
kids.nationalgeographic.com/animals/invertebrates/facts/black-widow

INDEX

biting, 18, 19
body parts, 5
eating, 8, 12, 14, 17
eggs, 10, 18
fangs, 16

homes, 6, 12
legs, 5, 15
mates, 8
predators, 12
prey, 15

silk, 12, 15, 17
size, 5
venom, 16, 19
webs, 10, 14, 15, 16

ABOUT THE AUTHOR

Lisa Amstutz is the author of more than 150 children's books on topics ranging from applesauce to zebra mussels. An ecologist by training, she enjoys sharing her love of nature with kids. Lisa lives on a small farm with her family.